INSIDE THE NFL

BUFFALO BILLS

by Charlie Beattie

Abdo & Daughters
MIDDLE GRADE NONFICTION

An imprint of Abdo Publishing
abdobooks.com

ABDOBOOKS.COM

Published by Abdo Publishing, a division of ABDO, PO Box 398166, Minneapolis, Minnesota 55439.

Printed in China.
052025
092025

Cover Photos: Michael Reaves/Getty Images Sport/Getty Images (Josh Allen); Allen Dean Steele/Getty Images Sport/Getty Images (Bruce Smith)
Interior Photos: Jerry Holt/Star Tribune/Getty Images, 4–5, 9; Hannah Foslien/Getty Images Sport/Getty Images, 6; Tom Pennington/Getty Images Sport/Getty Images, 7; Brett Carlsen/Getty Images Sport/Getty Images, 10, 51; Tom Szczerbowski/Getty Images Sport/Getty Images, 11; Abdo Publishing, 12–13; Bettmann/Getty Images, 14–15; AP Images, 16, 20; James Drake/Getty Images Sport/Getty Images, 17, 60 (bottom left); Brooks Kraft LLC/Sygma/Getty Images, 18; Focus on Sport/Getty Images, 19, 26, 28, 30, 35, 60 (top left); Herb Scharfman/Sports Imagery/Getty Images Sport/Getty Images, 21, 22; Focus on Sport/Getty Images Sport/Getty Images, 23, 38 (top); Tony Tomsic/AP Images, 24–25, 27; George Rose/Getty Images Sport/Getty Images, 29, 60 (top right); F. Carter Smith/AP Images, 31; Rick Stewart/Allsport/Getty Images Sport/Getty Images, 32, 45; Four Seam Images/AP Images, 33; Mark Lennthan/AP Images, 34; Al Bello/Allsport/Hulton Archive/Getty Images, 36–37, 60 (bottom right); Rick Stewart/Getty Images Sport/Getty Images, 38 (bottom); Al Messerschmidt Archive/AP Image, 39, 61 (top left); Paul Spinelli/NFL Photos/AP Images, 40, 61 (bottom left); George Gojkovich/Getty Images Sport/Getty Images, 41; John Hickey/AP Images, 42, 61 (top right); Gin Ellis/Getty Images Sport/Getty Images, 43; Stephen Dunn/Allsport/Getty Images Sport/Getty Images, 44; Jeff Haynes/AFP/Getty Images, 46; Matthew Stockman/Getty Images Sport/Getty Images, 48–49, 55; Brian Rothmuller/Icon Sportswire/Getty Images, 50; David Rosenblum/Icon Sportswire/Getty Images, 52, 63; Gregory Fisher/Icon Sportswire/Getty Images, 53; Leslie Plaza Johnson/Icon Sportswire/Getty Images, 54; Bryan M. Bennett/Getty Images Sport/Getty Images, 56; Jamie Squire/Getty Images Sport/Getty Images, 57; Shutterstock Images, 58; Jason Hanna/Getty Images Sport/Getty Images, 59, 61 (bottom right)

Editor: Chrös McDougall
Series Designer: Laura Graphenteen
Production Designer: Ryan Gale

Library of Congress Control Number: 2024948485

Publisher's Cataloging-in-Publication Data

Names: Beattie, Charlie, author.
Title: Buffalo Bills / by Charlie Beattie
Description: Minneapolis, Minnesota: Abdo Publishing, 2026 | Series: Inside the NFL | Includes online resources and index.
Identifiers: ISBN 9781098296650 (lib. bdg.) | ISBN 9798384919179 (ebook)
Subjects: LCSH: Buffalo Bills (Football team)--Juvenile literature. | National Football League--Juvenile literature. | Football teams--Juvenile literature. | American football--Juvenile literature.
Classification: DDC 796.333--dc23

CONTENTS

Buffalo Bills quarterback Josh Allen stretches the ball out for an early touchdown against the Minnesota Vikings in their 2018 game.

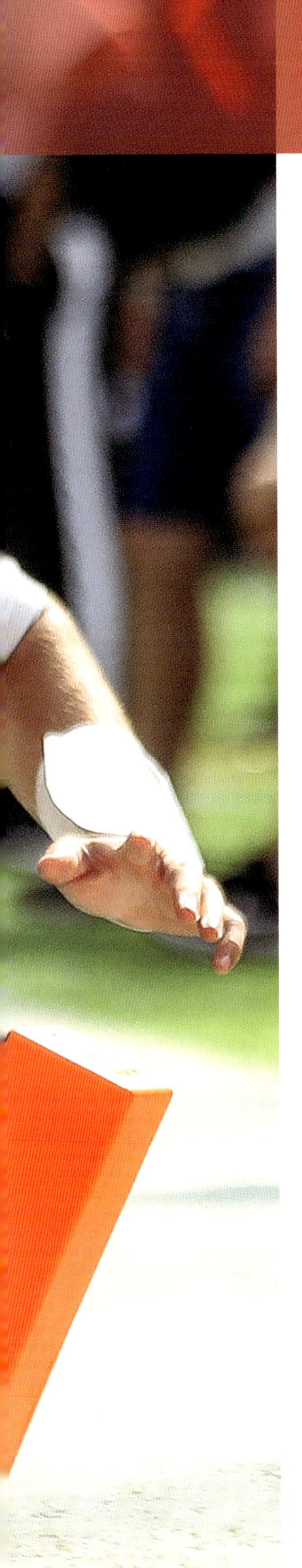

CHAPTER 1

ACROBATIC ALLEN

Facing second-and-long in the red zone, Buffalo Bills quarterback Josh Allen took the snap out of the shotgun. The rookie scanned the field. When he didn't spot an open receiver, Allen took off toward the left side. Anthony Barr, one of the Minnesota Vikings' star linebackers, was ready. He raced after the quarterback and then lunged with everything he had to tackle him. But Allen dived just a little farther. He reached out with the ball so it was barely inside the pylon for a Buffalo touchdown.

It was Week 3 of the 2018 National Football League (NFL) season. Fans weren't expecting much from the Bills or their rookie quarterback. Buffalo had started the season 0–2. Now the Bills were going against a strong Vikings team that had finished one win shy of the previous season's

Allen celebrates his first touchdown against Minnesota.

Super Bowl. But Allen, making only his second start, was out to show the football world what he was capable of.

UNKNOWN TALENT

Allen had been Buffalo's top draft pick in 2018. The young quarterback had not always been thought of as a top prospect, though. When he was coming out of high school in California, no top college teams wanted him. So, Allen went to a local junior college and tried to improve his standing. Following a strong season there, he wrote more than 1,000 letters to college coaches looking for an opportunity. Only Eastern Michigan and Wyoming offered the young hopeful a scholarship.

Allen moved to Laramie, Wyoming, and joined the Cowboys. In two seasons as the starting quarterback, he excelled on the field. The 6-foot-5-inch, 233-pounder combined a strong passing arm and good instincts as a runner. With each impressive game, his draft stock soared. By the time he was coming out of college, most scouts predicted he would be a first-round pick.

Allen was the highest draft pick to ever come out of Wyoming when the Bills selected him seventh in 2018.

That didn't mean that everyone thought he would be a star, though. Naysayers talked about Wyoming's weak schedule or the fact that Allen didn't always have the most accurate arm. Many expected that Allen would need some time to adjust to the NFL. That's what the Bills expected when they selected him seventh overall. However, when Buffalo starter Nathan Peterman struggled in Week 1, Allen came on in relief.

The rookie then got the call to start a Week 2 matchup against the Los Angeles Chargers. Though Buffalo lost 31–20, Allen threw his first career touchdown pass in the defeat. One week later, his touchdown drive against Minnesota gave the Bills an early 7–0 lead. And the rookie was just getting started.

A BIG JUMP

After the Vikings fumbled on their next drive, Buffalo added a field goal. Another Minnesota fumble gave Buffalo the ball at the Vikings' 27. Two plays later, Allen pump-faked to a receiver in the flat. He then lobbed a pass to a wide-open receiver down the field for a touchdown to make it 17–0. Playing in Minneapolis, the young Bills signal-caller had stunned the home crowd.

What Allen did next made the entire league take notice. Though many NFL quarterbacks can beat defenders on the run, most of them are smaller and leaner than Allen. He showed off those traits on Buffalo's next drive. The team faced third-and-nine at the Buffalo 36. Once again, Allen took off running. This time, he headed up the middle, and Barr was in his path. Instead of going around the 6-foot-5-inch linebacker, Allen lifted his left leg and hurdled Barr on his way to picking up the first down.

Legendary broadcaster Jim Nantz was calling the game on television. He spoke for many when he said, "How many quarterbacks have you seen hurdle anyone?"

"HOW MANY QUARTERBACKS HAVE YOU SEEN HURDLE ANYONE?"

—CBS SPORTSCASTER JIM NANTZ

Allen said he was "trusting my feet, trusting my gut," but really, he just wanted to get the first down.

Allen hurdles Vikings linebacker Anthony Barr on his way to picking up a first down for the Bills.

Minnesota came into the game favored to win by 17 points. The last time a team was expected to win by that much and lost had been in 1995. Yet, behind Allen's stunning play, Buffalo charged to a 17–0 first-quarter lead. Minnesota never recovered as the Bills went on to a shocking 27–6 upset win.

By the next day, Allen's leap had become a social media sensation. The Bills' communications team didn't miss a chance to promote their sudden star. For one post, they edited a photo of Allen so it looked as if he was hurdling a pair of live buffalo. Another post showed him leaping over the moon.

The Bills finished just 6–10 in 2018. Allen endured his share of typical rookie struggles. But he provided many more incredible moments as well. For the enthusiastic fans of Buffalo, the quarterback's hurdle served as a sign that their team was ready to grow by leaps and bounds.

IMPRESSING A LEGEND

Josh Allen's hurdle impressed many fans. But perhaps the most notable was former Bills quarterback Jim Kelly. The Hall of Famer was a legend in Buffalo for leading the team to four Super Bowl appearances. After the play, he posted online, "I know I never would have been able to hurdle like that. Well done!"

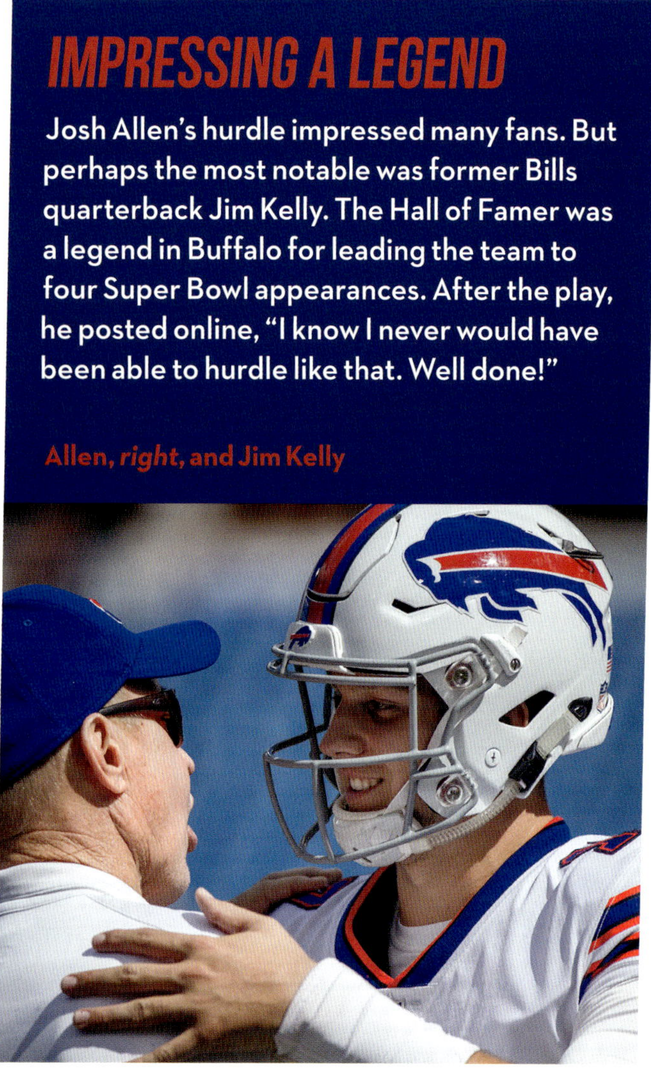

Allen, *right*, and Jim Kelly

Allen started 11 games in 2018 and threw for 2,074 yards along with 10 touchdowns.

NFL TEAMS MAP

NFC EAST	NFC WEST	NFC NORTH	NFC SOUTH
DALLAS COWBOYS	ARIZONA CARDINALS	CHICAGO BEARS	ATLANTA FALCONS
NEW YORK GIANTS	LOS ANGELES RAMS	DETROIT LIONS	CAROLINA PANTHERS
PHILADELPHIA EAGLES	SAN FRANCISCO 49ERS	GREEN BAY PACKERS	NEW ORLEANS SAINTS
WASHINGTON COMMANDERS	SEATTLE SEAHAWKS	MINNESOTA VIKINGS	TAMPA BAY BUCCANEERS

AFC

AFC EAST

- BUFFALO BILLS
- MIAMI DOLPHINS
- NEW ENGLAND PATRIOTS
- NEW YORK JETS

AFC WEST

- DENVER BRONCOS
- KANSAS CITY CHIEFS
- LAS VEGAS RAIDERS
- LOS ANGELES CHARGERS

AFC NORTH

- BALTIMORE RAVENS
- CINCINNATI BENGALS
- CLEVELAND BROWNS
- PITTSBURGH STEELERS

AFC SOUTH

- HOUSTON TEXANS
- INDIANAPOLIS COLTS
- JACKSONVILLE JAGUARS
- TENNESSEE TITANS

Ralph Wilson owned the Bills from 1960 until his death in 2014.

BORN IN BUFFALO

In the late 1950s, the NFL was surging in popularity. Business leaders all over the country were interested in founding new teams. But the existing NFL owners weren't interested in adding to the league. Undaunted, one group of prospective owners got together and decided to start a rival league. They called themselves "the Foolish Club" because taking on the NFL seemed like a crazy idea. That's how the American Football League (AFL) began.

The league had eight teams. One was set to play in Buffalo, New York. The team's owner, Ralph Wilson, had been a minority owner of the NFL's Detroit Lions in the 1950s. He didn't know much about Buffalo and decided to call his new team the Bills after legendary cowboy "Buffalo" Bill Cody.

The Bills played their home games in War Memorial Stadium from 1960 to 1972. The stadium was known as "the Rockpile" to players and fans.

Wilson also didn't know much about building a successful team. He admittedly wasn't an X's and O's football man. In putting together his team, the owner went with what he knew. Wilson hired a coach, Buster Ramsey, who had been an assistant with the Lions. Buffalo also signed up several players the Lions had cut. And when the Bills took the field in 1960, they did so wearing blue uniforms with silver helmets, just like the Lions did.

LOU, COOKIE, AND THE SENATOR

After stumbling to losing records in 1960 and 1961, the Bills reset. The team fired Ramsey and replaced him with Lou Saban for the 1962 season. The team's uniforms also changed to the familiar red, white, and blue the players still wear today.

Saban began bringing in new players to help improve the team. The first was powerful running back Carlton Gilchrist. Nicknamed "Cookie," Gilchrist used his 6-foot-3-inch, 250-pound frame to barrel through defenders. Gilchrist loved contact so much that even his teammates worried about being run over. Off the field, Gilchrist had a difficult personality. Coaches, including Saban, often struggled to deal with his mercurial nature.

Hard-charging running back Cookie Gilchrist led the AFL in rushing yards twice in three seasons with the Bills between 1962 and 1964.

Gilchrist led the AFL in rushing yards and touchdowns in 1962 as the Bills improved to 7–6–1. The next season, Saban nabbed a quarterback off the waiver wire to pair with his star runner. The San Diego Chargers had cut Jack Kemp after the quarterback injured his hand. Kemp signed with Buffalo and immediately became the starter. Teammates called Kemp "the Senator" for his studious nature, interest in politics, and leadership abilities. He proved to be a vital piece of Buffalo's winning puzzle.

TOUGH D

Led by Kemp and Gilchrist, the Bills charged out to a 9–0 start in 1964. But in a Week 10 loss to the Boston Patriots, the strongheaded Gilchrist grew frustrated that his coach wasn't giving him the ball. The star refused to go back into the game. An angry Saban kicked Gilchrist off the team the next day. It took an intervention from Kemp, who knew the team couldn't win without Gilchrist, to talk Saban into changing his mind.

The Bills and Patriots met again in the final week of the season with the division title on the line. Early in the game, Gilchrist demonstrated both his value and his toughness. He ran right over Boston defender Chuck Shonta, leaving the defensive back dazed. Gilchrist then walked into the Patriots' huddle and said, "Which one of you [guys] is next?" With Boston rattled, Buffalo rolled to a 24–14 victory and a spot in the AFL title game against San Diego.

Kemp wanted revenge against the team that had cut him. But it was Buffalo's exceptional defense that set the tone against the Chargers.

JACK KEMP GOES TO WASHINGTON

After his playing career, Jack Kemp became a respected politician. Despite his "Senator" nickname, he never served in the Senate. However, Kemp served as a US congressman representing western New York from 1971 to 1989. He later became a cabinet secretary under President George H. W. Bush. In 1996, Kemp was the Republican vice presidential nominee for Bob Dole.

Jack Kemp, *left*, and Bob Dole

Jack Kemp had a record of 43-31-3 in seven seasons as the Bills' starting quarterback.

Early in the game, San Diego quarterback Tobin Rote floated a pass for star running back Keith Lincoln in the left flat. As Lincoln stretched high to catch the ball, Bills linebacker Mike Stratton slammed into the running back's midsection with a hard, legal hit. Lincoln dropped the ball and had to leave the game injured.

For the rest of the game, the Bills shut down San Diego's high-powered offense for a 20–7 victory. Kemp capped things off with a 1-yard touchdown run in the fourth quarter. But after the game, teammates credited Stratton's big play. It became known as "the Hit Heard 'Round the World." San Diego coach Sid Gillman even praised Stratton. "That was one of the most beautiful tackles I have ever seen in my life," Gillman said.

"THAT WAS ONE OF THE MOST BEAUTIFUL TACKLES I HAVE EVER SEEN IN MY LIFE."

—SAN DIEGO CHARGERS COACH SID GILLMAN

Buffalo safety Hagood Clarke, *right*, breaks up a pass in a game against the Boston Patriots.

The AFL was known for its wide-open offenses. In Buffalo, the Bills instead locked teams down. In 1965, Buffalo had the league's best defense for the second straight season. Alongside Stratton, middle linebacker Harry Jacobs was the unit's heart. Behind them, defensive backs Butch Byrd, Hagood Clarke, Booker Edgerson, George Saimes, and Charley Warner had a combined total of 26 interceptions. All five earned a spot in the AFL's Pro Bowl that season.

Once again, the Bills reached the AFL title game to face the Chargers. Kemp threw an 18-yard touchdown pass to receiver Ernie Warlick in the first quarter to put the Bills up 7–0. In the second, Byrd received a punt and weaved 74 yards for a touchdown, putting Buffalo up 14–0. Groundbreaking "soccer-style" kicker Pete Gogolak added three field goals. Meanwhile, the defense dominated, with both Byrd and Jacobs picking off San Diego quarterback John Hadl to help Buffalo win 23–0.

Pete Gogolak (3) was one of the first "soccer-style" kickers in professional football. It is the same style that all kickers use today.

LESS THAN SUPER

Saban left the Bills after the 1965 title. Buffalo replaced him with Joe Collier, and the team didn't skip a beat. In 1966, the Bills once again boasted the league's best defense and won the AFL East title. That set up a matchup with the West champion Kansas City Chiefs. However, there was a new prize on the line. A year earlier, the NFL and AFL agreed to merge. The leagues were set to become one in 1970. Until then, they would meet in a postseason title game. So whoever won the AFL title would advance to the championship game that would later be called Super Bowl I.

Though favored against the Chiefs, the Bills stumbled. Kemp completed only 12 of his 27 passes and threw two interceptions in a 31–7 defeat. Instead of Buffalo, the Chiefs went on to represent

Bills defenders Mike Stratton, *left*, and Harry Jacobs, *right*, look to make a play against the Kansas City Chiefs in the AFL title game on January 1, 1967.

the AFL in the Super Bowl. Many dismissed the AFL as an inferior league, and that didn't change when the NFL powerhouse Green Bay Packers routed Kansas City 35–10. Several Bills players felt that they could have given the Packers a better game and therefore boosted the profile of the fledgling league.

THE JUICE

The aging Bills never reached those heights again. By 1968, the free-falling team had dropped to 1–12–1. Instead of competing for titles, the Bills were suddenly picking first in the 1969 draft. And that year, University of Southern California running back O. J. Simpson was the big prize. Nicknamed "Juice," Simpson had just won the prestigious Heisman Trophy as college football's top player. With his gliding, graceful style, Simpson was destined to be an NFL star, most observers thought.

Instead, Simpson endured two difficult seasons under coach John Rauch, who many felt didn't use the star back enough. Simpson didn't top 700 yards in 1969 or 1970 as the Bills won only seven total games. Before the next season, Rauch resigned, and Buffalo hired Harvey Johnson. Nothing changed for Simpson, who rushed for only 742 yards as Buffalo finished 1–13. What was once the great champion of the AFL had become a laughingstock in the newly merged NFL.

John Rauch directs play from the sidelines. Rauch went 7–20–1 in his two seasons as Buffalo's head coach in 1969 and 1970.

Bills running back O. J. Simpson finally topped the 1,000-yard rushing mark in his fourth season.

CHAPTER 3

BUFFALO PROUD

After three NFL seasons, O. J. Simpson was far from happy. The running back wanted to give up football. In 1972, a face from Buffalo's past returned, as the team brought Lou Saban back to become the head coach again. He immediately talked with Simpson and encouraged the back to stick it out.

"If you stay," Saban told the running back, "you just might like it."

Saban kept his word and made Simpson the focal point of Buffalo's offense in 1972. The tremendous runner was finally able to show what he could do. The Bills won only four games, but Simpson led the NFL with 1,251 rushing yards. In Week 7 against the Pittsburgh Steelers, Simpson broke loose for a 94-yard touchdown run. It was the longest run of his career and remained a Bills team record 50 years later.

THE ELECTRIC COMPANY

While Simpson thrived in 1972, he was historic the next year. In Week 1 of the 1973 season, Simpson ran for 250 yards and a pair of touchdowns against the New England Patriots. The Bills rode Simpson's rushing performance to a 9-5 record and came up just shy of a playoff spot. But the national spotlight stayed on Buffalo all year as "the Juice" continued to put up huge numbers.

With each game, Simpson's stardom grew. His offensive linemen decided to get in on the act as well. Tackles Dave Foley and Donnie Green, guards Reggie McKenzie and Joe DeLamielleure, and center Mike Montler dubbed themselves "the Electric Company." When asked why, they said it was because they turned on the juice.

Guard Reggie McKenzie, one of the leaders of "the Electric Company" offensive line, was an All-Pro each season from 1973 to 1976.

Heading into the final game of the season, Simpson

Buffalo center Mike Montler, *left*, looks to make a block for Simpson, *right*, during the running back's record-breaking game against the New York Jets in 1973.

needed 60 yards to break the NFL single-season rushing record of 1,863 yards. Striding gracefully despite the snowy field at New York's Shea Stadium, Simpson smashed that mark. With the record behind him, his teammates urged him to go for 2,000 yards. On his final run, Simpson ran off the left side and picked up five yards despite a Jets defender pulling on his face mask. Simpson finished with 2,003 yards for the year. Other runners have since reached the 2,000-yard milestone, but Simpson was the only player to do it in the era when teams played a 14-game season.

Simpson starred for three more seasons in Buffalo. He won additional rushing titles in both 1975 and 1976. Along the way, he became one of the country's most popular athletes. But the Bills reached the playoffs only once in Simpson's nine seasons and never won a postseason game. Buffalo let Simpson go before the 1978 season. After his career, he became a successful film actor and sportscaster. However, Simpson's playing career became overshadowed after he was accused of murdering his ex-wife and one of her friends in 1994. Though Simpson was found not guilty in a highly publicized trial, he wound up in legal trouble for the rest of his life.

Coach Chuck Knox had a record of 37–36 in five seasons with the Bills.

REBUILDING BUFFALO

By the time Simpson left the Bills, the team had fallen to last place again. Before the 1979 season, Buffalo made a splashy hire by bringing in Chuck Knox as the new head coach. Under Knox, the Los Angeles Rams had become regular contenders during the 1970s. Known as "Ground Chuck" for his fondness for running the football,

Running back Joe Cribbs (20) was named to the Pro Bowl three times in five seasons with the Bills.

Knox brought the Bills together with his disciplined attitude and fair treatment of his players.

By 1980, Knox had the Bills believing again. His players proved that when Buffalo knocked off the Miami Dolphins in the opener behind 131 total yards and a touchdown from star runner Joe Cribbs. The victory snapped a 20-game losing streak to the powerful Dolphins and spurred the Bills to a 5-0 start.

Though the team stumbled late, Buffalo traveled to San Francisco for the season final with a chance to reach the playoffs. In a driving rain, the Bills defense knocked down a late 49ers pass to preserve the victory and secure the team's first division title since 1966. However, the season ended when the Bills lost their playoff opener.

Behind a stingy defense built around nose tackle Fred Smerlas and linebacker Jim Haslett, the Bills went 10-6 in 1981

After struggling early in his career, quarterback Joe Ferguson became a prolific passer for the Bills in the late 1970s and early 1980s.

and reached the postseason as a wild card. Quarterback Joe Ferguson then threw two touchdown passes to build a 24–0 lead over the Jets in the playoff opener, and Buffalo held on to win 31–27. However, Buffalo's run ended a week later with a heartbreaking 28–21 loss to the Cincinnati Bengals.

A GIFT FOR THE OWNER

After Buffalo's streak-ending win over the Miami Dolphins in Week 1 of 1980, fans stormed the field. A group of supporters tore down the goalposts and hauled them up the stadium stairs. When they reached owner Ralph Wilson's private box, the fans presented their souvenir as a gift to the owner.

BUILDING A WINNER

Following back-to-back playoff berths, the Bills should have been a team on the rise.

Quarterback Jim Kelly angered Buffalo fans when he snubbed the Bills for the USFL in 1983.

Instead, Knox resigned in 1982 to take a job with the Seattle Seahawks. The Bills quickly plummeted in the standings again.

In 1983, the Bills searched for a new quarterback at the NFL Draft. With the 14th pick, they chose Jim Kelly. Kelly had a cannon for an arm and great toughness. He also wanted nothing to do with the Bills. Though Kelly had grown up in Pennsylvania, he had become accustomed to warm weather while attending the University of Miami. Playing in Buffalo's often cold, snowy conditions didn't appeal to the young quarterback. He instead signed with the Houston Gamblers of the new United States Football League (USFL).

For Bills fans, it was proof that no star players would ever come to Buffalo. But the Bills soon caught a few breaks. First, the team hired strong talent evaluator Bill Polian in 1984. At his first draft,

"HE IS SO STRONG THAT HE CAN BULLDOZE OVER YOU."

—WARREN MOON ON BRUCE SMITH

he snagged defensive end Bruce Smith with the first overall pick. Smith was a devastating force on defense. In his Hall of Fame career, Smith became the NFL's all-time leader in sacks. "He is so strong that he can bulldoze over you," said Hall of Fame quarterback Warren Moon.

Smith was a no-brainer pick in the top spot. But in the fourth round, Polian nabbed receiver Andre Reed from tiny Kutztown University in Pennsylvania. Few thought the small-school pass catcher would become an NFL star. Instead, Reed eventually retired as the Bills' all-time leading receiver. And when Reed left the game, only two players in league history had more catches.

Wide receiver Andre Reed had at least 1,000 receiving yards four times in 15 seasons with the Bills.

The Bills promoted Polian to general manager prior to the 1986 season. Buffalo also got some good fortune that summer when the USFL folded and Kelly signed with the Bills. The team finally had its quarterback. And after a 2–7 start, Polian changed coaches too. He fired Hank Bullough and hired Marv Levy. The 61-year-old was a strange choice. His only NFL head coaching experience had been a failed tenure with the Kansas City Chiefs from 1978 to 1982. Though he'd led a USFL team in 1984, Levy sat out the 1985 season. But the coach, who loved to quote classic works of literature in his pep talks, proved to be a great leader for the Bills.

THE BICKERING BILLS

Levy turned Buffalo's cold weather into a badge of honor for the players. As the team broke huddles before games, Levy used to say, "Where would you rather be than right here, right now?" The slogan became a team mantra that is still used in Buffalo.

Meanwhile, Polian continued to acquire more talent. In 1987, he added key defensive players in linebacker Shane Conlan and cornerback Nate Odomes.

Marv Levy coached the Bills from 1986 to 1997.

Defensive end Bruce Smith swats down a pass in a win against the Houston Oilers in the playoffs after the 1987 season.

A year later, Buffalo drafted shifty running back Thurman Thomas with its top pick. Thomas became the Bills' all-time leading rusher on his way to the Hall of Fame.

Things finally came together in Thomas's rookie season of 1988 when the Bills won 12 games. Though they fell one step shy of the Super Bowl, the Bills appeared to be championship contenders. Instead, the Bills fell back to 9–7 the next season. During the year, Kelly suffered a shoulder injury and blamed his offensive line. Throughout the year, teammates and coaches blamed one another for the team's failures. The local press dubbed Buffalo

Bills running back Thurman Thomas rushed for at least 1,000 yards every season from 1989 to 1996.

"the Bickering Bills." While the Bills still made the playoffs, they lost their first game. The team appeared to have great potential. In order to reach it, though, the Bills needed to get on the same page.

Quarterback Jim Kelly's 35,467 passing yards and 237 touchdowns were team records when he left the Bills.

CHAPTER 4

SUPER BOWL HEARTBREAKS

BY DECEMBER 1990, THE BILLS HAD COME TOGETHER AS A TEAM AND surged to a 9–2 start. They came out against the Philadelphia Eagles in Week 13 with a new wrinkle on offense. The Bills didn't huddle. And instead of relaying plays in from the sideline, the coaches let veteran quarterback Jim Kelly call his own plays at the line of scrimmage. The Bills raced from play to play against the bewildered Eagles defense. At the end of the first quarter, Kelly had completed all eight of his passes for 229 yards. Buffalo led 24–0. The Bills held on to win the game 30–23, and the "K-Gun" offense was born.

Buffalo lost only once the rest of the season. In the playoffs, the K-Gun took off to an even greater level. The Bills piled up 493 offensive yards in a 44–34 win over the Miami Dolphins.

Running back Thurman Thomas (34) looks to turn the corner during the Bills' victory over the Miami Dolphins in the divisional playoffs after the 1990 season.

Then they totaled 502 yards of offense to rout the Los Angeles Raiders 51–3 and earn a spot in Super Bowl XXV.

WIDE RIGHT

In their first Super Bowl, the Bills squared off against the New York Giants. With their powerful defense, the Giants slowed down the K-Gun by dropping several players back to stop the pass. New York also held the ball for most of the game, keeping Kelly and the Bills' offense stuck on the sideline.

Kelly celebrates a Bills touchdown in Super Bowl XXV after the 1990 season.

Even still, Buffalo trailed only 20–19 when it got the ball with 2:16 left. Kelly ran for 18 yards on that drive, and star rusher Thurman Thomas added 33. With eight seconds left, the Bills had the ball at the New York 29. Kicker Scott Norwood trotted onto the field with a chance to win it. He put enough power behind his kick. However, the ball drifted wide of the right upright, sealing defeat for the Bills.

Bills kicker Scott Norwood connects with his fateful missed field goal in the final seconds of Super Bowl XXV.

THE MISSING HELMET

The defeat in Super Bowl XXV didn't slow down the Bills. In 1991, Thomas racked up more than 1,400 yards rushing and another 651 receiving, all while scoring 12 touchdowns. He earned NFL Most Valuable Player (MVP) honors.

After thumping the Kansas City Chiefs in the divisional round, Buffalo gutted out a rare low-scoring game against the Denver Broncos for the AFC title. The Bills' only touchdown came in the third quarter, when cornerback Carlton Bailey intercepted a pass and took it 11 yards to the end zone. Norwood, who had been embraced by the city despite his big miss a year earlier, added a field goal that proved to be the difference in a 10–7 win.

Bills defensive tackle Phil Hansen walks off the field after Buffalo's loss to Washington in Super Bowl XXVI on January 26, 1992.

In their return trip to the Super Bowl, the Bills defense held Washington on its first series. But when the Bills offense went to take the field, Thomas couldn't find his helmet. The star back's headgear was missing for only a few plays, but the mishap set the tone for Super Bowl XXVI as the Bills lost 37–24.

THE COMEBACK

On the final day of the 1992 season, the Houston Oilers rocked the Bills 27–3. The loss cost Buffalo a division title. Even worse, Kelly strained ligaments in his knee. When the Bills and Oilers met again the following weekend for a wild-card matchup, Buffalo's star had to watch from the frozen sideline at the team's Rich Stadium.

Longtime backup Frank Reich took Kelly's place. But early in the game, the Bills watched as Houston's Warren Moon tossed four touchdown passes. Buffalo could answer with only a single field goal. The Bills fell behind even further when Reich threw an interception early in the third quarter that the Oilers returned for a touchdown. The Bills were now down 35–3. No team had ever come back from a deficit that large in an NFL game.

Reich had once led the largest comeback in college football as a senior at Maryland. And on this day, he shook off the interception and led two quick scoring drives sandwiched around an onside kick. By the 7:46 mark of the third quarter, Buffalo had pulled back to 35–17.

STEVE TASKER

Wide receiver Steve Tasker caught only 49 passes in 12 seasons with the Bills after joining the team in 1986. But many of his teammates think Tasker belongs in the Hall of Fame. The 5-foot-9-inch receiver was an ace on special teams. In his career, Tasker made 204 special teams tackles and blocked seven punts. He made the Pro Bowl seven times and became the first special teams player to win Pro Bowl MVP when he took home the honor in 1993.

Steve Tasker (89) blocks a punt in a 1988 game.

Quarterback Frank Reich threw for 289 yards and four touchdowns in Buffalo's comeback win over the Houston Oilers.

The Bills then forced a quick punt and marched down the field for another touchdown. On Houston's next drive, Buffalo's Henry Jones intercepted a pass deep in Houston territory. On fourth-and-five, Reich hit Andre Reed on an 18-yard touchdown pass. In a span of 6:52, the Bills had cut Houston's lead to four points, 35–31.

When the score was 35–3, many of Buffalo's fans had gone home. After hearing the comeback on their car radios, some raced back and reentered the stadium. They made it back in time to see Buffalo go ahead with 3:08 left on a 17-yard pass from Reich to Reed. Though Houston tied the game and forced overtime, Bills kicker Steve Christie won it 41–38 on the Bills' first overtime possession.

The game became known simply as "the Comeback." It remains a legendary moment in Buffalo. Coach Marv Levy later joked about the number of fans who claimed they were there, stating, "70,000 people were at that game. I've already met 400,000 of them."

The Bills rode the momentum of the comeback to their third straight Super Bowl. There, they met the Dallas Cowboys, who were becoming an NFL power. Dallas overwhelmed Buffalo 52–17. Despite the lopsided defeat, the Bills still made the game's most memorable play. Late in the fourth quarter, with the game already decided, Dallas defensive lineman Leon Lett recovered a fumble and raced more than 50 yards toward the end zone. He slowed down near the goal line to showboat without realizing that Buffalo receiver Don Beebe was chasing him down. Beebe forced a fumble, preventing a touchdown. The play didn't mean much to the outcome, but it showed the spirit of the Bills.

Bills receiver Don Beebe, *left*, chases down Dallas's Leon Lett to force a fumble late in Super Bowl XXVII in January 1993.

END OF THE LINE

By 1993, many NFL fans had grown tired of seeing the Bills reach the Super Bowl. But the Bills didn't let up. They won the AFC East and beat the Raiders and Chiefs to reach the Super Bowl against Dallas again. This time, the Bills led 13–6 at halftime. However, early in the third quarter, Thomas fumbled at the Bills' 46. Dallas recovered and raced the ball in for a touchdown to tie the game. From there, the Bills crumbled as the Cowboys won 30–13.

The Super Bowl loss was Buffalo's fourth. That tied the Bills with the Broncos and Minnesota Vikings for the most in history. And by losing four straight, Buffalo had become a national punch line.

After missing the playoffs in 1994, the Bills lost in the divisional round a year later. It was clear the team was getting old. The team bounced back by winning another division title in 1996. However, the visiting Jacksonville Jaguars upset the Bills in the wild-card round. Late in the game, Kelly suffered a concussion and had to be carted off the field. That ended up being the final moment of the 36-year-old quarterback's NFL career.

Levy left a year later, following a 6–10 season. Reed, Thomas, and Bruce Smith all stayed with the Bills under new head coach

A Bills fan holds a hopeful sign before Super Bowl XXVIII in January 1994.

Thomas hangs his head on the sidelines late in Buffalo's loss in Super Bowl XXVIII.

Bills quarterback Doug Flutie, *left*, and linebacker John Holecek react to the Titans' "Music City Miracle" in the playoffs after the 1999 season.

Wade Phillips. They helped Buffalo bounce back to 10–6 and return to the playoffs. However, the Bills fell on the road to the Dolphins in the wild-card round.

The playoff loss stung. What happened the next season stung even more. Following an 11-win season, Buffalo traveled to Nashville to take on the Tennessee Titans in the wild-card round. It was a tight game. Finally, with 16 seconds remaining, Christie made a long field goal to put Buffalo up 16–15. The Titans needed a miracle in order to come back with so little time left. Yet, that's what happened.

Tennessee's Lorenzo Neal fielded the kickoff around the 25-yard line. He took a few steps to the right and handed the ball off to teammate Frank Wycheck. The Titans tight end continued toward the right sideline before stopping, turning around, and throwing a lateral across the field to Kevin Dyson. The wide receiver caught the ball near the left sideline and then took off. Bills defenders chased after him, but it was no use. Dyson ran the kickoff 75 yards for a shocking winning score.

The NFL later ranked "the Music City Miracle" as the fourth greatest play in league history. There was no celebrating in Buffalo, though. The Bills' season was over. And soon after, Smith and Thomas left for new teams, while Reed retired. Just like that, Tennessee's unlikely trick play brought an end to a joyous yet painful period in Bills history.

Drew Bledsoe became the first Bills quarterback to throw more than 4,000 yards in a season when he threw for 4,359 in 2002.

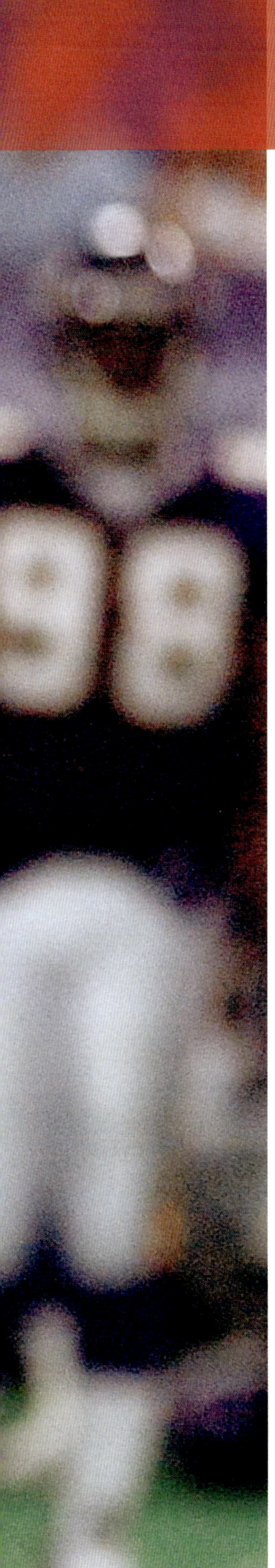

CHAPTER 5

BACK TO THE TOP

Throughout the early 2000s, Bills fans were treated to a handful of memorable performances, but the Bills churned through quarterbacks, struggling to find the right signal-caller to lead the team. Only one, veteran Drew Bledsoe in 2004, led Buffalo to a winning record. The team finished 9–7 but missed the playoffs. The 32-year-old Bledsoe left the team that offseason.

In 2009, the Bills brought in journeyman quarterback Ryan Fitzpatrick to back up the team's young starter, Trent Edwards. Fitzpatrick had already played for two teams after the St. Louis Rams drafted him in the seventh round out of Harvard in 2009. Buffalo fans weren't expecting a star. However, after Edwards struggled, Fitzpatrick got his chance and ran with it. In one of his first starts, he threw a 98-yard touchdown pass against the Jacksonville Jaguars. It was the longest play in Bills history.

Fitzpatrick could be an erratic performer. In four seasons with the Bills, he threw 64 interceptions, including a league-high 23 in 2011. But he also thrilled fans with his gunslinging mentality and ability to make exciting plays.

One of Fitzpatrick's greatest moments came against the New England Patriots in 2011. New England came in having won 15 straight against Buffalo and went up 21–0 in the first half. Fitzpatrick, who tossed two interceptions early, rebounded to throw for 369 yards and a pair of touchdowns. The Bills hit a field goal as time expired to win 34–31. After that comeback, Fitzpatrick's thrilling plays became known as "Fitzmagic."

Though Fitzpatrick brought excitement, even he couldn't lift the Bills back into contention. In Fitzpatrick's four years, the Bills never finished better than 6–10. Fitzpatrick brought his exciting play to six more

BILLS MAFIA

In 2010, Bills receiver Stevie Johnson dropped a potential game-winning touchdown pass in a Week 10 game. Afterward, several fans shared their support for the player online with the hashtag "Bills Mafia." Three Buffalo fans—Breyon Harris, Del Reid, and Leslie Wille—took the term further. They created an official fan group and named it after the hashtag. Today, the Bills Mafia is known for its passionate devotion to the team and players as well as its pregame tailgate parties on home game days.

Bills coach Sean McDermott gets fired up after a defensive stop in a 2017 game.

NFL teams before retiring after the 2021 season, but his "magic" was born in Buffalo.

A COACH AND A QUARTERBACK

By 2017, the Bills had missed the playoffs in 17 consecutive seasons, the longest streak in the NFL. Before the season started, the Bills hired Sean McDermott as head coach. The former defensive coordinator was the 10th different sideline boss the team had brought in since Marv Levy had left in 1997.

In 2017, McDermott led a scrappy Bills team into Miami to face the Dolphins on the last day of the season. The Bills were 8–7 and needed a win for a shot at the playoffs. Buffalo built a 22–3 lead

Bills defensive end Jerry Hughes prepares for a snap in the team's wild-card playoff game against the Jacksonville Jaguars in January 2018.

and hung on for a 22–17 win. Buffalo still needed help, though. When the Baltimore Ravens lost later that day, the Bills' long playoff drought had ended.

The season came to an end a week later with a 10–3 loss to the Jaguars in the playoffs. Despite making the postseason, the Bills had been a weak offensive team. McDermott and general manager Brandon Beane drafted quarterback Josh Allen in 2018 to change that.

Allen became a fan favorite right away in Buffalo. In addition to his all-action style on the field, the young quarterback embraced the underdog city. Despite growing up 3,000 miles (4,800 km) away in California, Allen said he didn't mind New York's cold winters.

Quarterback Josh Allen runs for a touchdown during the Bills' comeback against the New York Jets in 2019.

And he converted fans instantly when, before the draft, he talked up Buffalo's famous spicy chicken wings as one of his favorite foods.

KINGS OF THE EAST

Buffalo missed the postseason in Allen's rookie year as the young quarterback had ups and downs. But he provided the team's fans with enough hope that he could be the team's best passer since Jim Kelly. Even Kelly endorsed the rookie's talent.

That potential showed in the 2019 season opener when Allen led a comeback from 16–0 on the road against the New York Jets. With three minutes left, he lofted a 38-yard game-winning score to receiver John Brown. That was one of four fourth-quarter comebacks Allen led during a thrilling season.

Buffalo cornerback Tre'Davious White takes down Houston receiver DeAndre Hopkins in the teams' wild-card round matchup in January 2020.

Buffalo finished 10-6 and reached the playoffs as a wild card. But the postseason brought familiar disappointment as the Bills built a 16–0 first-half lead on the Houston Texans only to crumble after halftime and lose 22–19 in overtime.

For most of the 2000s, the AFC East had belonged to star quarterback Tom Brady and the Patriots. But when Brady left New England in 2020, the Bills saw their opportunity. Allen delivered his finest season yet. He threw 37 touchdown passes and ran for eight more. He teamed up with three excellent receivers in the sure-handed Cole Beasley and deep threats Gabe Davis and Stefon Diggs. After leading the Bills to a 13–3 record and their first division title in 25 years, Allen finished as the runner-up for the NFL MVP Award.

Wide receiver Stefon Diggs led the NFL with 127 receptions for 1,535 yards in 2020. Both totals were also Buffalo records.

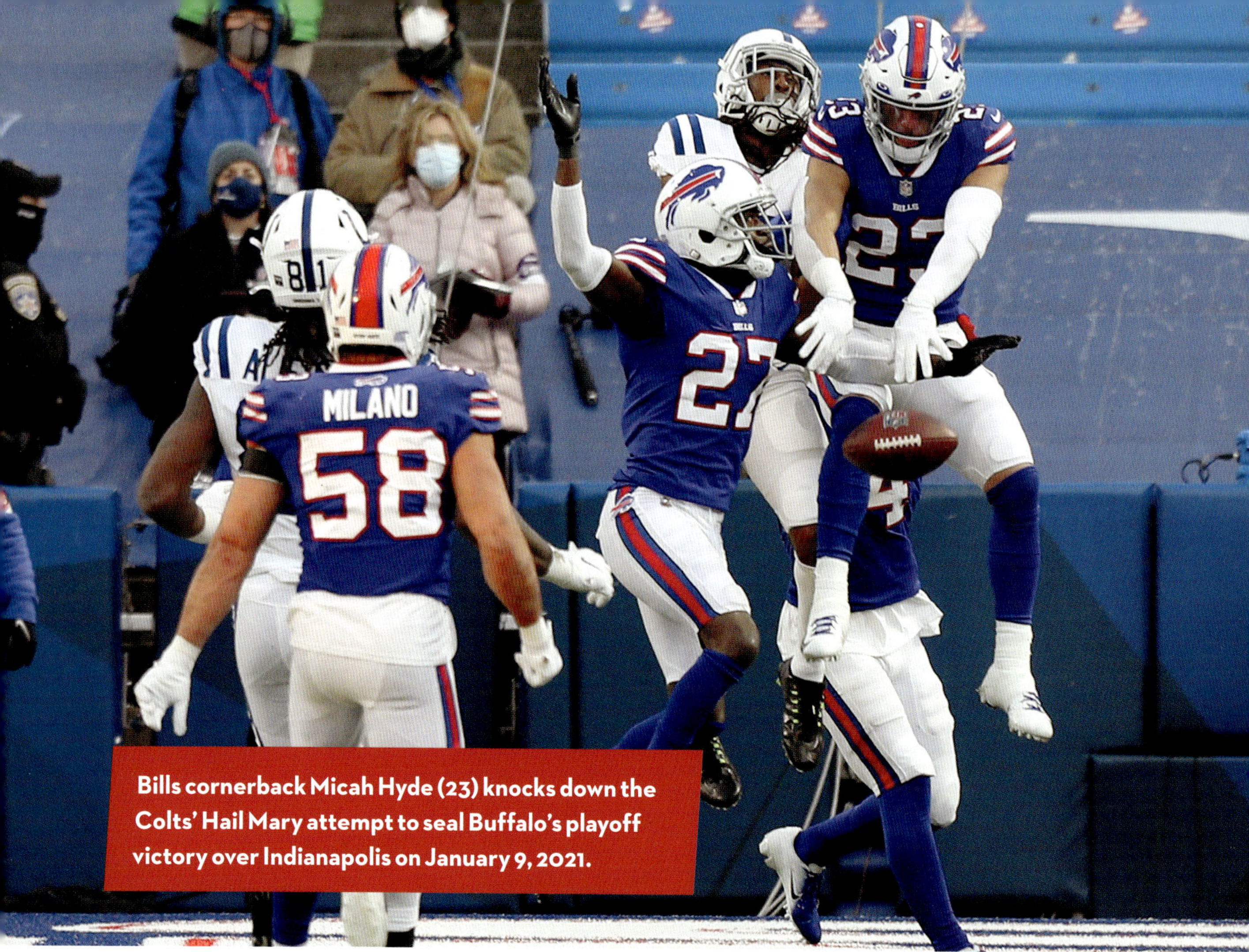

Bills cornerback Micah Hyde (23) knocks down the Colts' Hail Mary attempt to seal Buffalo's playoff victory over Indianapolis on January 9, 2021.

The next step for the young quarterback was to deliver playoff success. And he did just that in a thrilling 27–24 win over the visiting Indianapolis Colts in the wild-card round. Allen threw a pair of touchdown passes and ran for a third score. The Bills' defense knocked down a last-second Hail Mary attempt to seal the win. The Bills followed that up with a shutdown defensive performance, beating the Baltimore Ravens 17–3.

Those wins set up a matchup with the defending Super Bowl champion Kansas City Chiefs in the AFC title game. It proved to be an epic quarterback battle between Allen and the Chiefs' Patrick Mahomes, but the Chiefs came out ahead 38–24.

ALLEN VS. MAHOMES

The Bills and Chiefs met again early in the 2021 season. Allen got revenge by totaling four touchdowns in a 38–20 win. But the rivalry was only heating up. Buffalo traveled to chilly Kansas City for a showdown in the divisional round of the playoffs. In a back-and-forth game, the Chiefs led 26–21 with two minutes to play.

Bills receiver Gabe Davis, *right*, and running back Devin Singletary celebrate Davis's go-ahead touchdown with 13 seconds left in the divisional playoffs against the Kansas City Chiefs in January 2022.

What followed was one of the most exciting two-minute stretches in football history. Allen threw a pair of touchdown passes. But Mahomes matched the Bills quarterback with heroics of his own. The Chiefs won the game 42–36 in overtime. The loss was heartbreaking for Bills fans.

The team didn't get past the divisional round in the 2022 or 2023 season either, losing to the Chiefs again in the latter. Buffalo made some

SUPER BOWL CHAMPIONSHIPS: 0

AFL CHAMPIONSHIPS: 2

1964, 1965

CONFERENCE CHAMPIONSHIPS: 4

1990, 1991, 1992, 1993

DIVISION TITLES: 15

AFL East: 1964, 1965, 1966
AFC East: 1980, 1988, 1989, 1990, 1991, 1993, 1995, 2020, 2021, 2022, 2023, 2024

All stats are through the 2024 season.

big changes that offseason. Many people expected the team to take a step back in 2024. Allen refused to let that happen. In Week 11, his late 26-yard rushing touchdown secured a win over the undefeated Chiefs. Three weeks later, he threw for three touchdowns while

Allen earned his first NFL MVP Award after totaling 41 touchdowns in 2024.

running for three more. That had never been done before. Behind the highest-scoring offense in Bills history, the team finished 13–4 and won a fifth straight AFC East title.

After opening the playoffs with wins over the Denver Broncos and Baltimore Ravens, Buffalo traveled to Kansas City to take on the defending champion Chiefs. With a trip to the Super Bowl on the line, Mahomes led his team to a 21–10 first-half lead. Then, Buffalo came charging back as Allen threw for two touchdowns and running back James Cook ran for his second. But once again, the Bills fell just short, losing 32–29. It was another bitter postseason disappointment for Buffalo. But with Allen running the show, the future was still bright for Bills fans.

TIMELINE

The Bills are founded as part of the new AFL.
1960

The Bills defeat the Chargers 23-0 to win back-to-back AFL championships.
1965

The Bills win their first playoff game in 15 years by beating the New York Jets 31-27 on December 27.
1981

1964
Buffalo wins its first AFL title with a 20-7 victory over the San Diego Chargers on December 26.

1973
Bills star O. J. Simpson becomes the first running back to top 2,000 yards in a season.

1983
Buffalo picks Jim Kelly in the first round of the NFL Draft. He rejects the Bills to play in the USFL.

The Bills lose Super Bowl XXV 20-19 to the New York Giants on January 27.

1991

The Bills pull off the largest comeback in NFL playoff history against the Houston Oilers on January 3 but lose in the Super Bowl for a third straight year.

1993

The Bills lose "the Music City Miracle" to the Tennessee Titans on January 8 and don't return to the playoffs for 18 years.

2000

1992

Buffalo loses its second straight Super Bowl, this time 37-24 to Washington on January 26.

1994

Despite leading 13-6 at halftime, the Bills lose Super Bowl XXVIII to the Dallas Cowboys 30-13 on January 30.

2024

Quarterback Josh Allen is named NFL MVP after leading the Bills to their fifth consecutive AFC East title.

GLOSSARY

contender–a person or team that has a good chance at winning a championship.

coordinator–an assistant coach who is in charge of the offense, defense, or special teams.

draft–a system that allows teams to acquire new players coming into the league.

era–a period of time in history.

general manager–an executive who runs a team and is responsible for finding and signing players.

Hail Mary–a long pass that has a small chance of succeeding, usually made near the end of a game as a last-ditch effort to score.

journeyman–a player who has played for many teams or has been unable to find a specific role.

lateral–a pass that goes sideways or backward.

mercurial–prone to rapid and unpredictable mood changes.

merge–join with another to create something new, such as a company, a team, or a league.

minority owner–someone who owns a small percentage of a team.

overtime–an extra period of play when the score is tied after regulation.

prospect–an athlete likely to succeed at the next level.

retire–to end one's career.

rival–a peer that is competing to be the best in a particular field.

rookie–a professional athlete in his or her first year of competition.

sack–a tackle of the quarterback behind the line of scrimmage before he can pass the ball.

scholarship–money provided to a student-athlete to pay for his or her education.

scout–a person whose job is to look for talented young players.

shotgun–a formation in which the quarterback lines up 5 to 7 yards behind the center and takes the snap in the air.

upset–an unexpected victory by a supposedly weaker team or player.

veteran–someone who has played for many years.

waiver wire–a list of players who have been cut. Teams can submit a claim to sign one of these players.

wild-card–the first round of the playoffs.

To learn more about the Buffalo Bills, please visit **abdobooklinks.com** or scan this QR code. These links are routinely monitored and updated to provide the most current information available.